LESSONS
OF FAITH & GRACE

Stories of Life, Lessons of Faith,
Reminders of God's Unfailing Love

Annette Richardson

Copyright © 2025 by Annette Richardson.
Wake Forest, NC

All rights reserved. No part of this book may be reproduced or used in any manner without written permission of the copyright owner except for the use of quotations in a book review.

First hard back edition October 2025.

Book Project Management by
Raindrop Creative, Inc. | StartWrite Publish Team

Editor:
Tiara Brown

Cover Art:
Raindrop Design Team

ISBN: 978-1-970179-18-7 (Hardback)

For more information, email address:
richardsona1022@gmail.com

FIRST EDITION

Unless otherwise noted, all Scripture references or quotations are from the English Standard Version of the Bible and marked ESV. The ESV Global Study Bible®, ESV® Bible

Copyright © 2012 by Crossway.

All rights reserved.

Dedication

I dedicate this book first to my Heavenly Father. Without Him, these words would have no meaning, and this journey would have no purpose.

To my beloved mother, Patricia, my queen, my encourager, and my greatest earthly example of faith. Your words, your prayers, and your unwavering trust in God continue to guide me even as you rest in His arms. This book is as much your story as it is mine, for your legacy of love and devotion to Christ lives on in me.

To my children, Jordan and Cydney, who are my joy and inspiration. May these stories remind you always to walk with Jesus, to live with courage, and to trust God in every season of life.

And to every reader who opens these pages, may you find encouragement, strength, and hope in these stories. My prayer is that you will experience the unfailing love of God and be reminded that His mercies are new every morning.

Table of Contents

Dedication 3
Introduction: Where Faith Meets Grace 7
Chapter 1: Lessons from a Mother's Faith 9
    Angels Among Us 10
    Do Well 13
    Growing Through Grief 16
    Unshakeable Promises 19
    The Day the Sunshine Went Away 22
    When Time Stood Still 25
    You Better Let That Mess Go 28
    Your Eyes are Beautiful 31

Chapter 2: Everyday Lessons of Faith 35
    Bless the Cheese 36
    No Shortcuts with God 39
    Shower Cries 42
    God Chose Me, Fleas and All 45
    Dare to Be Different 48
    Lessons From the Passenger's Seat 51
    Hakuna Matata (No Worries) 54
    Highway Grace 57
    The Gentle Power of Humility 60
    The Coffee Mug: When Love Pours Over 63
    When Pressure Becomes Purpose 66
    Trust Him with the "Soccer Turn" 69

    When Apples Fall 72
    Finding Strength in Connection 75

Chapter 3: Strength and Grace in Trials 79
    Faith That Moves Mountains 80
    It Is Part of the Process.. 83
    Breaking and Becoming.. 86
    It's the Piercing for Me 89
    The Gift of Laughter: God's Medicine for the Soul 92
    Finding Shalom... 95
    The Missing... 98

Chapter 4: Faithful Stewardship 101
    Temple Maintenance 102
    Parenting Through the Seasons 106
    Seeds of Access 110

Chapter 5: Celebrating God's Goodness 115
    Love "Agape" Style... 116
    The Climb and the Promises 119
    The Golf Clap 122
    Open Hands, God's Plans 125
    I Am Proud Of You.. 128

Author's Message 131

Introduction:
Where Faith Meets Grace

This book is a collection of stories birthed out of life experiences, lessons from my family, and most importantly, my relationship with Jesus Christ. Each page holds a piece of my story, the joys, the struggles, the grief, the laughter, and the everyday moments where God showed His faithfulness.

Much of my faith was shaped by the influence of my mother. She was my sunshine, my encouragement, and my prayer warrior. Her words, her wisdom, and her unwavering trust in the Lord continue to guide me even though she now rests with Him. Many of the stories in this book reflect the lessons she lived out: lessons of forgiveness, grace, strength, doing well, and letting go. Through her example, I learned what it means to walk with Jesus in every season of life.

You will notice each story contains a Scripture passage introduced with the phrase *"My Bible Reads."* This simple phrase is intentional. It reflects the personal way I engage with God's Word, as though I am holding it close and allowing it to speak directly into my life.

My prayer is that as you read, you will see your own story woven into God's story. Whether you are navigating grief, seeking joy in everyday life, enduring trials, celebrating God's goodness, or reflecting on His grace, may you be reminded that His promises are true, His mercies are new every morning, and His love never fails.

This book is not just about my journey; it is an invitation for you to pause, reflect, and experience the presence of God in your own life. So, pour yourself a cup of tea, find a quiet corner, and open your heart. My hope is that these stories will encourage you, strengthen your faith, and remind you that you are deeply loved by the One who holds every detail of your life in His hands.

CHAPTER 1:
Lessons from a Mother's Faith

Our mothers often become our first
teachers of faith, kindness, and strength.
In the following stories, lessons learned from a
mother's life and legacy are revealed.
Her words, her example, and even her absence
have taught me how to live with purpose,
grieve with hope, and cling to God's promises.
May these stories remind you of the gift of
spiritual inheritance and inspire you to honor
the legacy of faith in your own family.

ANGELS AMONG US

My Bible reads: *"For he will command his angels concerning you to guard you in all your ways."* - Psalm 91:11, ESV

Reflection

In the final days with my mother, I gently said to her, "Mama, you look so beautiful–you are glowing." She smiled, looked past me, and asked softly, "Annette, do you hear that music?"

I answered, "No, Mama, I do not hear the music."

She closed her eyes and rested back in her chair, serene and calm. In that sacred moment, I knew she was in the presence of angels, heavenly escorts ushering her straight into the presence of God. My mother was seeing into a realm I could not yet see.

God is so generous, faithful, and loving that He sends His angels to comfort us, protect us, and help us in times of need. Psalm 91 reminds us that God gives His angels charge over us to keep us in all our ways. They fight battles we cannot see, protect us from harm, and bring encouragement when we feel alone.

My Bible also reads, "Do not neglect to show hospitality to strangers, for thereby some have entertained angels unawares" (Hebrews 13:2). These verses remind us to live with kindness and openness to others, because God's presence often shows up in the ordinary moments, sometimes even through angelic encounters.

Today, I am grateful for the angels God has assigned to my life. I rest in knowing that I am never alone, and neither are you.

Prayer:

Lord, thank You for loving me so much that You send angels to watch over me. Help me to trust Your protection and guidance, even when I cannot see it. Teach me to show kindness to others, knowing that I may be entertaining angels without even realizing it.

Amen

Lessons of Faith and Grace

Reflecting Questions:

1. Have there been moments in your life when you felt God's angels were protecting, guiding, or comforting you—even if you couldn't see them?
2. How does knowing God sends His angels to watch over you change the way you face fear or uncertainty?
3. How might remembering that God's angels are active in both seen and unseen ways give you courage to face today's challenges with greater peace?

DO WELL

My Bible reads: *"And let us not grow weary of doing good, for in due season we will reap, if we do not give up."*- Galatians 6:9, ESV

Reflection

It has been nearly a year since my mother went home to be with the Lord, and I still find myself reflecting on her life and character. My mother did many things well. She lived well, loved well, gave well, and forgave well.

She was not perfect, but she consistently strived to do what was right. I watched her give out of her lack, love people even when it was not easy, and quietly bless others when no one was watching. Since her passing, I have heard countless stories of the lives she touched, testimonies of her kindness, generosity, and faith. Her life reminds me that doing good is rarely convenient, but it is always worth it.

Galatians 6:9 urges us not to grow weary in well-doing, promising that our faithful efforts will one day bear fruit. Doing well means living out the fruit of the Spirit, kindness, love, joy, peace, patience, faithfulness, gentleness, self-control, and goodness; even when it is difficult. When life becomes discouraging, exhausting, or confusing, we can lean on God for strength and direction. Proverbs 3:5-6 reminds us to trust in the Lord with all our heart and acknowledge Him in all we do, and He will make our paths straight.

My mother's life was a living example of this truth. Now, she is resting at the feet of Jesus, and I believe she is smiling down, trusting that her seeds (the lives she impacted) will continue to do well.

I challenge you today: live well, love well, give well, and forgive well. Life is too short to do anything less than well.

Prayer:

Father, thank You for the people who have gone before us and shown us what it looks like to live well. Strengthen me when I grow weary, guide me when I am uncertain, and teach me to live, love, give, and forgive in a way that honors You.

Amen

Reflecting Questions:

1. My mother modeled living, loving, giving, and forgiving well. Which of these four areas is God inviting you to grow in more deeply right now?
2. Galatians 6:9 encourages us not to grow weary in well-doing. When do you find it most difficult to keep doing good, and how can you draw strength from God in those moments?
3. Proverbs 3:5-6 calls us to trust in the Lord with all our heart. How can trusting God's direction help you continue doing well when life feels overwhelming or confusing?

GROWING THROUGH GRIEF

My Bible reads: *"Two are better than one, because they have a good reward for their toil. For if they fall, one will lift up his fellow. But woe to him who is alone when he falls and has not another to lift him up!"*
- Ecclesiastes 4:9-10, ESV

Reflection

Friday, May 31, 2019, marked the first anniversary of my mother's passing. She was not only my mother but also my best friend. This past year has been a journey of learning, healing, and growing through grief.

Grief is one of those trials that God allows to shape us into His image. It is painful, but it is also purposeful. Each wave of sorrow has taught me something about God's faithfulness and His comfort.

One of the most important lessons I've learned is the value of having an inner circle–people I can trust to walk with me through the hard days. Jesus had an inner circle, and I believe we are called to have one too.

I have allowed my inner circle to see me vulnerable and broken–the version of me that is still under construction. They have loved me at my worst, accepted my quirks, corrected me when I was wrong, spoken life to me, and shown me grace.

Satan wants us isolated because when we are alone, our struggles can consume us, and no one knows how to pray for us. But God designed us for community. We need others to help us stand when we fall, encourage us when we are weak, and remind us of the truth when we forget it.

Grief is hard, but we do not have to walk through it alone. And even in grief, God is working, shaping us, and drawing us closer to Him.

Prayer:

Lord, thank You for walking with me through my grief and for placing people in my life to love, support, and lift me. Help me to open my heart to others, to let them in, and to allow them to be Your hands and feet in my life. Heal my heart and teach me to comfort others with the same comfort I have received from You.

Amen

Lessons of Faith and Grace

Reflecting Questions:

1. How has grief, whether through the loss of a loved one, a job, or another change, shaped your relationship with God? In what ways has He met you in your brokenness?
2. Ecclesiastes 4:9–10 reminds us of the importance of an inner circle. Who are the people in your life that help lift you when you fall, and how can you nurture those relationships?
3. Grief can either isolate us or grow us. What intentional steps can you take to let others into your journey, so that God's love and comfort can flow through them to you?

UNSHAKEABLE PROMISES

My Bible reads: *"For all the promises of God find their Yes in him. That is why it is through him that we utter our amen to God for his glory."*
- 2 Corinthians 1:20, ESV

Reflection

On May 31, 2018, at 3 a.m., I received the call I had been expecting but dreaded. My younger sister said the words I wasn't ready to hear: "She's gone." My mother, my best friend, had gone home to be with her Lord and Savior. Though I knew it was coming, my heart still felt unprepared.

Just a week later, on June 7, I stood at her funeral and shared words God gave me to honor her life. I remembered the strength of her faith, the way she stood firmly on God's Word and His promises. She knew that whether in healing on earth or eternal healing in heaven, she was in a *win-win* situation: "If I die, I am with Jesus, and if I stay here, I am with Him too."

Lessons of Faith and Grace

Mama lived with faith, hope, and love:

1. **Faith** — knowing without it, it is impossible to please God.
2. **Hope** — believing in what she could not see.
3. **Love** — living out Jesus' command to love one another.

Her life was marked by grace. Even in her suffering, she prayed, *"Lord, I thank You for cancer,"* because she trusted God's purposes. His promises sustained her. His grace empowered her. His love carried her home.

When I think about my mother, I am reminded that God's promises never fail. Healing may not always look like what we expect, but His "yes" and His "amen" are eternal. His promises are life, peace, hope, and salvation.

Prayer:

Lord, thank You for Your unfailing promises. Thank You for giving me an example of faith and perseverance through my mother's life. Teach me to stand on Your Word, to trust Your promises even in the darkest seasons, and to believe that Your grace is always sufficient.

Amen

Annette Richardson

Reflecting Questions:

1. 2 Corinthians 1:20 says, "For all the promises of God in Him are Yes, and in Him amen" Which of God's promises have you held onto most tightly during seasons of trial, and how have they sustained you?
2. Who in your life has lived with unwavering faith in God, and how does their example encourage you to trust God's promises more fully in your own life?
3. When life feels uncertain or overwhelming, how can you remind yourself daily that God's promises are unshakeable?

THE DAY THE SUNSHINE WENT AWAY

My Bible reads: *"But we do not want you to be uninformed, brothers, about those who are asleep, that you may not grieve as others do who have no hope. For since we believe that Jesus died and rose again, even so, through Jesus, God will bring with him those who have fallen asleep."*
- 1 Thessalonians 4:13–14, ESV

Reflection

My aunt used to call my mother her "sunshine." I imagine she was sunshine to so many others as well. Her smile could brighten any room, her presence was a breath of fresh air, and her joy was contagious.

When my mother passed, it felt as though my sunshine had gone away. The grief was excruciating. I missed everything: our playful quarrels, our bursts of laughter, our late-night talks over snacks, and our spontaneous shopping trips. Life felt cloudy, heavy, and dim.

Ecclesiastes 11:7 reminds us, "Truly light is sweet, and it is pleasant for the eyes to behold the sun." Sunshine brings warmth, life, and hope. And though the day felt dark when my sunshine went away, God, in His faithfulness, allowed me to experience light again. He comforted me, walked with me in the valley of grief, and reminded me that in Christ, sorrow does not have the final word. The blessed assurance of 1 Thessalonians 4:13–14 gives me hope: I will see my sunshine again. Death does not end the story; it is simply a doorway into eternity with Jesus.

Prayer:

Lord, thank You for the gift of my sunshine; the people You place in our lives who brighten our days. Thank You for comforting me when grief felt overwhelming and for restoring joy to my heart. Help me to live in hope, trusting Your promise that one day, we will be reunited with those who rest in You.

Amen

Reflecting Questions:

1. Grief often feels like the absence of light. In what ways have you experienced God bringing new "sunshine" or moments of joy even in seasons of deep sorrow?
2. 1 Thessalonians 4:13–14 reminds us that we do not grieve as those without hope. How does the promise of reunion with loved ones in Christ shape the way you carry your grief today?
3. Who in your life has been a source of "sunshine" during your hardest days, and how can you thank God for them or reflect His light to someone else in need?

WHEN TIME STOOD STILL

My Bible reads: *"But now thus says the Lord,*
he who created you, O Jacob,
he who formed you, O Israel:
"Fear not, for I have redeemed you;
I have called you by name, you are mine."
- Isaiah 43:1, ESV

Reflection

In 1974, the Rolling Stones released a song titled *"Time Waits for No One."* Most days, time feels like a rushing river, steady, constant, unstoppable. But there are moments when time seems to stop: when life itself feels suspended.

For me, that moment came on May 31, 2018, the day my mother went home to be with Jesus. Nearly a year later, it still felt like yesterday. Time moved swiftly on the calendar, but for me, it stood still. That day was the longest, most devastating day of my life.

Her smile, our talks, our laughter, even our mother-daughter quarrels, all of it suddenly came to an end. My heart was both comforted and crushed: grateful that she was resting in the arms of Jesus, but aching because I longed for her presence with me.

Psalm 34:18, ESV reminds us: "The Lord is near to the brokenhearted and saves the crushed in spirit." In those stagnant moments when time stood still, God's presence held me together. He strengthened me, wiped my tears, and calmed my fears with His love.

Time did not wait for me, but it did not need to wait for my mother either. She was ready for her appointed time, prepared to step into eternity with her Heavenly Father. And in that, I find peace—knowing He held both of us in His hands.

Prayer:

Lord, thank You for being near when time seems to stand still. Thank You for comforting my broken heart and reminding me that Your love is constant through the passage of time. Help me to trust Your timing, rest in Your promises, and rejoice in the hope of eternal life.

Amen

Annette Richardson

Reflecting Questions:

1. Looking back on moments when time seemed to stop in your own life, how did God meet you in your grief, fear, or uncertainty?
2. Psalm 34:18 says, "The Lord is near to the brokenhearted and saves the crushed in spirit." How have you experienced this nearness of God in seasons of heartbreak?
3. Have you experienced a family member who was prepared to meet their heavenly Father? How did their readiness encourage you to live each day with eternity in view?

YOU BETTER LET THAT MESS GO

My Bible reads: *"Let all bitterness and wrath and anger and clamor and slander be put away from you, along with all malice. Be kind to one another, tenderhearted, forgiving one another, as God in Christ forgave you."* - Ephesians 4:31–32, ESV

Reflection

I vividly remember conversations with my mother about the ways people mistreated me or tried to defame my character. She would listen patiently, sometimes with tears in her eyes, but she always gave me the same response: *"The Lord knows. Annette, you'd better let that mess go."*

Her words were never focused on what was done to me, but on how I chose to respond. That simple phrase has stayed with me for years, because it was her way of teaching me the necessity of forgiveness.

Unforgiveness is like untreated heart disease; it slowly damages us from the inside. But when we forgive, we allow God to step in as the "heart regulator." He restores what was broken and sets our hearts back in rhythm with His. As 1 Peter 5:7 reminds us, we have the privilege of casting all our cares, hurts, and offenses on Him, because He cares for us.

Forgiveness doesn't excuse the wrong done to us. Instead, it frees us. It loosens the grip of bitterness and resentment, allowing us to live with peace and joy. As the Huffington Post once noted, forgiveness is about releasing ourselves; not about letting the other person off the hook.

The cross is our ultimate example. How can we withhold forgiveness when God grants it to us daily? There is power, healing, and freedom in forgiveness. Sometimes the wisest thing we can do is exactly what my mother said: *"...let that mess go."*

Prayer:

Lord, thank You for forgiving me daily through the sacrifice of Jesus Christ. Teach me to release offenses, to let go of bitterness, and to walk in the freedom of forgiveness. Be my heart regulator and help me to love others the way You love me.

Amen

Reflecting Questions:

1. What "mess" (bitterness, unforgiveness, or offense) are you still holding onto that God is inviting you to release to Him today?
2. 1 Peter 5:7, ESV reminds us to cast, "... all your care upon Him, for He cares for you." What practical step can you take this week to cast your burdens onto God instead of carrying them yourself?
3. How does remembering God as the ultimate "heart regulator" encourage you to forgive others quickly and keep your heart free from damage?

YOUR EYES ARE BEAUTIFUL

My Bible reads: *"The eye is the lamp of the body. So, if your eye is healthy, your whole body will be full of light,"* - Matthew 6:22, ESV

Reflection

In February of 2018, my mother looked at me with love and said, *"Your eyes are beautiful."* At first, I responded with a simple "thank you," but later I pondered the depth of her words. Perhaps she was not only acknowledging the outward beauty of my eyes but also speaking to the uniqueness of my soul. Maybe, as mothers often do, she was looking deeper, knowing there would come a day when she would no longer be able to look into my eyes again.

Scripture reminds us that our eyes are more than just physical features–they are lamps to our bodies. They reflect what resides within us and reveal whether we are filled with light or darkness. What we choose to let into our eyes will inevitably shape our hearts and flow out into our lives.

For example, David described himself as the apple of God's eye (Psalm 17:8, ESV); a phrase that signifies being precious, protected, and cherished by the Lord. Just as a mother tenderly watches over her child, our

Heavenly Father guards us with His gaze, shielding us from harm and guiding us with love.

I am grateful for the gift of my eyes, not only for what they allow me to see in the world but also for what they remind me about God's care and my mother's affirmation. To hear her say, *"Your eyes are beautiful,"* was a reminder that beauty flows from the soul and that when we are rooted in Christ, His light radiates through us.

Prayer:

Lord, thank You for being the One who sees me completely. Help me to guard my eyes so that my heart remains pure and full of Your light. May others see Your beauty reflected through me, just as my mother once did.

Amen

Reflecting Questions:

1. Matthew 6:22, ESV says, "The eye is the lamp of the body..." What are you allowing into your eyes and heart that either fills you with God's light or clouds your soul with darkness?
2. The author's mother's words pointed not only to the beauty of her eyes but also to the beauty of her soul. How do you want your life to "shine through your eyes" so that others see Christ in you?
3. In Psalm 17:8, David describes himself as "the apple of God's eye." How does knowing that God sees you as precious and worthy of His protection change the way you view yourself?

Lessons of Faith and Grace

CHAPTER 2:
Everyday Lessons of Faith

God is not confined to pulpits or church pews. He shows up in kitchens, on highways, at soccer fields, and in everyday conversations. In the following stories, ordinary moments that have revealed extraordinary truths about God are shared. Each story will encourage you to see divinity woven into the details of your daily life, teaching us to trust Him with even the smallest things.

BLESS THE CHEESE

My Bible reads: *"And my God will supply every need of yours according to his riches in glory in Christ Jesus."* - Philippians 4:19, ESV

Reflection

"Bless the cheese," my dad would say. As a child, I remember thinking it was a strange thing to say; after all, who blesses cheese? Years later, I wrote to my dad asking if he remembered saying this to us. He wrote back with laughing faces and said, "Yes!"

But the blessing was never about the cheese. My dad was teaching us to be thankful, to recognize that every good thing we had, no matter how small, came from God.

Sometimes we take life's daily provisions for granted: a simple meal, a roof over our heads, or the little moments that bring joy. But when we pause to give thanks, we shift our focus from the gift to the Giver. As Colossians 3:17 reminds us, "Whatever you do, in word or deed, do everything in the name of the Lord Jesus, giving thanks to God the Father through Him."

Gratitude transforms ordinary moments into worship. It reminds us that Jesus, the Bread of Life, is the One who provides our daily bread, both physically and spiritually. So today, "bless the cheese," and thank God for the big and small blessings in your life. Each one is a reminder of His love and faithfulness.

Prayer:

Father, thank You for being my provider. Help me to see Your hand in every part of my life, in the small blessings and the big ones. Teach me to live with a grateful heart and to remember that every good gift comes from You.

Amen

Lessons of Faith and Grace

Reflecting Questions:

1. What "small" blessings (things you might overlook) in your daily life, can you pause and thank God for today?
2. Philippians 4:19 reminds us that God will supply all our needs. How can practicing gratitude for even the simplest provisions strengthen your faith in His promises?
3. How does shifting your focus from the *gift* (the cheese) to the *Giver* (God) transform the way you approach prayer and thanksgiving?

NO SHORTCUTS WITH GOD

My Bible reads: *"Enter by the narrow gate. For the gate is wide and the way is easy that leads to destruction, and those who enter by it are many."*
- Matthew 7:13, ESV

Reflection

If you were anything like me in high school or college, you might have used *Cliff's Notes* to get through some of those long reading assignments. These pamphlets provided summaries of classic works of literature, giving us just enough information to pass the quiz–or so we thought. But the truth is, *Cliff's Notes* could never capture the author's full intention, tone, or emotional depth. Reading these summaries caused us to miss out on the richness of the original story.

And life can be like that too. Sometimes we want the shortcut–the easy route, the fast track, the "Cliff's Notes version" of spiritual growth. But God doesn't work that way. He takes us through a process; one that takes time, endurance, and trust.

2 Timothy 2:12, ESV reminds us, "if we endure, we will also reign with him." Our endurance is evidence of our faithfulness. Every challenge we face is an oppor-

tunity to know God more deeply–not just know *about* Him.

When we resist shortcuts and stay on the path God has set for us, we experience the fullness of His plan. And just like finishing a great book, we come away with a deeper understanding and appreciation for the Author of life.

Prayer:

Lord, help me resist the temptation to take shortcuts in my faith journey. Teach me to trust Your process, even when it feels long or difficult. I want to know You more deeply, to grow through every season, and to endure so that I may reign with You.

Amen

Reflecting Questions:

1. In what areas of your life are you tempted to take "shortcuts" instead of trusting God's process, and what might He be teaching you through the waiting?
2. Matthew 7:13 warns against the easy, shortcut path. How can you choose the narrow road of obedience, even when it feels longer or harder?
3. Looking back, how has persevering through a full "process" (instead of cutting corners) produced deeper faith, character, or wisdom in your life?

SHOWER CRIES

My Bible reads: *"You have kept count of my tossings; put my tears in your bottle. Are they not in your book?"* - Psalm 56:8, ESV

Reflection

After my mother passed away, the shower became the place where my tears fell the heaviest. It became my refuge, my hiding place, where I could release the grief that I tried so hard to contain in front of others. The sound of rushing water masked my sobs, and the steam wrapped around me like a fragile blanket. Shower cries became my norm.

Grief has a way of showing up in unexpected places. Sometimes it's loud and public, and other times it's quiet and tucked away behind closed doors. Yet even in those hidden moments, God is present. Scripture tells me that God noticed every tear I cried in the shower. None were wasted.

When the water mingled with my tears, I often thought of how cleansing grief can be. Though painful, it softens our hearts, reminds us of our dependence on God, and opens us to His comfort. My Bible reads, "Blessed are those who mourn, for they shall be comforted" (Matthew 5:4, ESV). The comfort doesn't always come immediately, but it is *sure*. His presence in those hidden places is proof of His existence.

Now, when I think back to those moments, I realize that the shower was more than a place of grief. It was an altar. It was where I met God in my rawest state, no mask, no pretending, just me and Him. He was faithful to meet me there every single time.

Prayer:

Lord, thank You for being the God who collects every tear I cry. When my heart feels too heavy and the grief too deep to carry, remind me that I am never alone in my sorrow. You see me, You hear me, and You comfort me even when words cannot form. Wrap me in Your peace when waves of emotion come and strengthen me to trust You through the pain. Turn my tears into testimonies of Your faithfulness, and let Your love wash over me like healing rain.

Amen

Lessons of Faith and Grace

Reflecting Questions:

1. Where do you find yourself releasing your deepest grief? Have you allowed God to meet you in that space?
2. How does knowing that God collects your tears bring you comfort in seasons of sorrow?
3. Can you identify a time when hidden moments of grief turned into moments of unexpected worship?

GOD CHOSE ME, FLEAS AND ALL

My Bible reads: *"...but God shows his love for us in that while we were still sinners, Christ died for us"*
- Romans 5:8, ESV

Reflection

On August 15, 2018, I went to the animal shelter to pick out our dog. When I first saw him, he smelled horrible and was covered in fleas. But something in my heart knew this was the dog God meant for us to have.

We scheduled a vet appointment for the very next day. At the veterinarian's office, he was cleaned, treated, and prepared to come home with us. Our dog, Common, is still learning and adjusting to his new life, but he belongs to us, fleas and all.

As I reflect on this, I am grateful that God did the same for me. When I was "smelly" with sin, messy, and broken, He did not throw me away. He chose to love me in my condition and began the process of transforming me into who He created me to be.

Romans 3:23, ESV reminds us, "for all have sinned and fall short of the glory of God." None of us are perfect, and yet God meets us right where we are. He washes us clean, heals our wounds, and teaches us how to walk in His ways.

This is also how we are called to treat others. The people God places in our lives will not always have it all together. Some will be hurting, struggling, or "covered in fleas." Our job is not to judge or discard them, but to love them and trust God to work in their lives, just as He continues to work in ours.

Prayer:

Lord, thank You for loving me at my worst and choosing me when I was broken and unworthy. Help me extend that same grace and patience to others. Teach me to see people through Your eyes, to love them in their mess, and to trust You to bring healing and transformation in their lives.

Amen

Annette Richardson

Reflecting Questions:

1. Romans 5:8 says, "While we were yet sinners, Christ died for us." How does this truth change the way you see yourself in light of God's unconditional love?
2. God loved you even in your "messy" moments. How can you extend that same grace and acceptance to others who may not look, act, or live the way you think they should?
3. What "fleas" (struggles, flaws, or weaknesses) in your life are you tempted to hide, and how can surrendering them to God open the way for His healing and transformation?

DARE TO BE DIFFERENT

My Bible reads: *"But you are a chosen race, a royal priesthood, a holy nation, a people for his own possession, that you may proclaim the excellencies of him who called you out of darkness into his marvelous light."* - 1 Peter 2:9, ESV

Reflection

In a world where everyone seems to want to blend in or copy someone else, it's easy to forget that being different is not just okay, it's a calling. For example, I remember when my daughter was in kindergarten. She came home upset because her classmates had made fun of her clothes. I gently reminded her of the importance of being "different."

I often use Jesus and even Punky Brewster as examples when I talk to my children about standing out. As Christians, we are called to be "peculiar people." We are not meant to blend in with the world. Our words, actions, and even the way we love others should reflect the God we serve.

Being different might mean being misunderstood. It might mean being teased, judged, or left out. But that's okay, because our goal is not to fit in with the world, but to reflect the light of Christ. So, when someone calls you strange or mocks you for living by a different standard, rejoice. You are living out your calling. You are standing out for Jesus.

Prayer:

Lord, thank You for choosing me and calling me Your own. Help me to live boldly for You, even when it means being different from the world around me. Give me the courage to stand out and reflect Your light wherever I go.

Amen

Lessons of Faith and Grace

Reflecting Questions:

1. 1 Peter 2:9 calls us a *"chosen generation, a royal priesthood, a holy nation, a peculiar people."* In what ways do you feel God calling you to stand apart from the world?
2. When have you felt pressured to "blend in," and how did you respond? How might remembering that your identity is in Christ give you courage to remain faithful?
3. How can you model for others, especially children or those you influence, that being "different" for Christ is not a burden, but a blessing?

LESSONS FROM THE PASSENGER'S SEAT

My Bible reads: *"I will instruct you and teach you in the way you should go; I will counsel you with my eye upon you."* - Psalm 32:8, ESV

Reflection

A few months ago, I began the exciting yet daunting task of teaching my daughter how to drive. Watching her excitement and growing confidence has been a joy. The challenging part, however, is the lack of control. My role is simply to guide, offer practice opportunities, and trust her to obey my instructions.

One thing became clear during this process: the main thing standing between us and an accident is my voice and her obedience. This display is a picture of our relationship with God. As our Heavenly Father, He provides guidance, instruction, and opportunities to grow. He does not take control of the "wheel" by force; instead, He invites us to trust His voice and follow His direction.

Isaiah 41:10 reminds us not to fear because God is with us, strengthening and helping us. Psalm 25:4-5, ESV is a prayer that reads, "Make me to know your ways, O Lord; teach me your paths. Lead me in your truth and teach me, for you are the God of my salvation; for you I wait all the day long." When we let God lead, He will never steer us wrong. But when we resist, ignore His Word, or "veer off course," we put ourselves in danger. God's Word is like the rules of the road designed not to limit us but to protect us and keep us safe.

Just like my daughter must trust me to guide her into becoming a safe driver, we must trust our Heavenly Father to lead us into His best for our lives. His direction is always right, and His love never fails.

Prayer:

Lord, thank You for guiding me through every twist and turn in life. Help me to trust Your voice and follow Your Word. Teach me to release control, to stay on the path You've set for me, and to find peace knowing You are with me every step of the way.

Amen

Reflecting Questions:

1. Just as learning to drive requires trust in the instructor and attentiveness to the road, what does it mean for you to fully trust God as your guide on life's journey?
2. When was the last time you tried to "take the wheel" in your own strength instead of letting God lead? What did you learn from that experience?
3. How can you practice being more attentive to God's "road signs" (His Word, the Holy Spirit's nudges, or wise counsel), so you stay on the right path?

HAKUNA MATATA (NO WORRIES)

My Bible reads: *"do not be anxious about anything, but in everything by prayer and supplication with thanksgiving let your requests be made known to God. And the peace of God, which surpasses all understanding, will guard your hearts and your minds in Christ Jesus."* - Philippians 4:6–7, ESV

Reflection

When *The Lion King* premiered in 1994, the song *Hakuna Matata* quickly became a joyful anthem. The phrase means "no worries," and its upbeat rhythm and playful message captured hearts across generations.

As I think about Hakuna Matata today, I realize how powerful it can be when we apply it through the lens of faith. God invites us to trade our worry for His peace. Worry doesn't change the outcome; it only steals our joy. But when we pray, trust, and release our concerns to God, He promises to guard our hearts and minds.

Isaiah 26:3, ESV reminds us, "You keep him in perfect peace whose mind is stayed on you, because he trusts in you." Our Heavenly Father is omniscient and omnipotent; nothing takes Him by surprise. Just as He faithfully provides for the birds of the air, He promises to take care of us.

Hakuna Matata isn't just a catchy phrase—it can be a lifestyle of faith. Choosing peace over worry, trust over fear, and prayer over anxiety allows God's joy to flood our hearts and minds.

Prayer:

Lord, thank You for the gift of peace that surpasses all understanding. Teach me to cast my cares on You and live without worry. Help me to focus on Your promises and trust Your perfect plan for my life.

Amen

Reflecting Questions:

1. What are the worries or anxieties in your life right now that God is inviting you to release into His hands?
2. Philippians 4:6–7 promises peace when we bring our requests to God with thanksgiving. How can you practice this in your daily routine so that "Hakuna Matata–no worries" becomes more than a phrase, but a way of life?
3. When was the last time you experienced God's peace in a situation where you would normally have been anxious? What did that moment teach you about trusting Him more fully?

HIGHWAY GRACE

My Bible reads: *"and are justified by his grace as a gift, through the redemption that is in Christ Jesus."*
- Romans 3:24, ESV

Reflection

On August 25, 2018, I was traveling home from my sister's house when I became dangerously sleepy behind the wheel. I found myself twirling my hair, something I always do when exhaustion sets in, and I could feel my eyes start to close. Twice I had to pull over to nap: once for five minutes, and once for a full hour (the best nap!). I was so grateful that I stopped, instead of pushing through and risking my life or someone else's.

Every time I get on the road, I pray for "highway grace," God's protection and guidance while I travel. That day reminded me that God always gives us choices. He doesn't force us to do anything. We can make foolish decisions that put us and others in danger, or we can choose wisely and allow His grace to protect us.

The same is true in life. Grace is God's gift, undeserved and unearned. His grace covers our mistakes, redeems our foolishness, and empowers us to live differently. Grace is not an excuse to keep living recklessly but an invitation to transformation.

Lessons of Faith and Grace

Jesus is persistent. Even when we resist, He keeps showing up, offering love, forgiveness, and a new way of living. Eventually, grace draws us into communion with Him so we can stop "driving sleepy" through life, searching for fulfillment in the wrong places.

God's grace is amazing, but it also carries responsibility. He disciplines those He loves because He wants us to "get it right." How we live matters. Grace isn't just about forgiveness; it's about being empowered to live for Him.

Prayer:

Lord, thank You for Your amazing grace that covers my life. Thank You for protecting me, even when I've made poor choices. Help me to receive Your grace not as an excuse to keep sinning, but as the power to live differently. Saturate my life with Your presence and guide me safely to the destination You have prepared for me.

Amen

Reflecting Questions:

1. Think of a time when you made a wise choice that protected you from harm. How did God's grace meet you in that moment, even if the outcome could have gone another way?
2. Grace is God's undeserved gift to us. In what areas of your life do you most need to lean on His grace right now: habits, relationships, or decisions?
3. How does recognizing God's grace in your daily choices inspire you to live more carefully and intentionally for Him?

THE GENTLE POWER OF HUMILITY

My Bible reads: *"Do nothing out of selfish ambition or vain conceit, but in humility consider others better than yourselves."* - Philippians 2:3

Reflection

In the 1939 film *The Little Princess*, Shirley Temple portrays Sarah, a young girl who goes from privilege to poverty. Though she loses her wealth and position, she never loses her character. Sarah's humility is shown in how she befriends Becky, a servant girl, and continues to share kindness and generosity, even when her own circumstances change.

Her example reminds us that humility isn't weakness, it's strength under control. It is the ability to love, serve, and forgive, even when treated unfairly. My Bible also reads, "Do not let any unwholesome talk come out of your mouths, but only what is helpful for building others up according to their needs" (Ephesians 4:29).

Humility means relying on God rather than our own strength. It means putting others ahead of ourselves, creating peace where there could be strife, and responding to injustice with love rather than bitterness. True humility doesn't seek recognition; it reflects the heart of Christ.

When situations don't go the way we expect, we can remember that there are no failures in Christ. Choosing humility is choosing victory, because it shows we belong to Him.

Prayer:

Lord, thank You for the example of humility shown in Christ, who came not to be served but to serve. Teach me to put others first, to speak words that build up, and to love even when I'm treated unfairly. Help me to walk in humility, knowing that in You, there are no failures.

Amen

Reflecting Questions:

1. Sarah, in *The Little Princess,* chose kindness and service even when her status changed. How can you show humility and compassion when life does not go the way you expected?
2. Humility is not weakness but strength under God's control. In what ways can you rely less on your own strength and more on God's power in your daily life?
3. Think of someone who has wronged you. How might humility guide your words and actions toward that person in a way that honors Christ?

THE COFFEE MUG: WHEN LOVE POURS OVER

My Bible reads: *"The steadfast love of the Lord never ceases; his mercies never come to an end; they are new every morning; great is your faithfulness."*
- Lamentations 3:22–23, ESV

Reflection

In 2016, my mother gave me a coffee mug as a gift of gratitude during her illness. The mug is simple, painted in white and light blue, with butterflies fluttering across its inside and outside. On the side, in black cursive letters, are these words: *"The Lord's mercies are new every morning."*

I use this mug only a couple of times each week, but each time I do, it carries a deeper meaning than any ordinary dish. It reminds me of my mother's love, her gratitude, and most importantly, the unending mercies of God.

Every morning is a chance to begin again. With each sunrise, God paints a fresh canvas of grace. His mercies come in the breath we draw, the warmth of sunshine, the nourishment of rain, and the resilience He gives us to face trials. Even on days when we feel weary or overwhelmed, His compassions never fail.

The coffee mug is more than a keepsake; it's a daily reminder that because of His great love, we are not consumed. God is for us, not against us. His faithfulness is constant, His mercies inexhaustible, and His love unconditional. Each sip reminds me that yesterday's mistakes are erased and today is a new beginning.

Prayer:

Lord, thank You for Your mercies that are new every morning. Help me to embrace each day as a fresh start, resting in Your faithfulness and Your unconditional love. May even the simplest objects in my life remind me of Your presence and grace.

Amen

Annette Richardson

Reflecting Questions:

1. Each morning, God gives us fresh mercies (Lamentations 3:22–23). How does this truth shape the way you begin your day, especially after a difficult night or season?
2. The coffee mug from my mother became a daily reminder of God's faithfulness. What objects or simple daily practices in your life point you back to His goodness?
3. When you think about starting over with a "clean slate," what past worries or failures do you need to release so you can embrace the new mercies God offers today?

WHEN PRESSURE BECOMES PURPOSE

My Bible reads: *"For this light momentary affliction is preparing for us an eternal weight of glory beyond all comparison."* - 2 Corinthians 4:17, ESV

Reflection

Few things frustrate me more than when the tire pressure light comes on in my car. I know it means my safety, fuel efficiency, and even the life of my tires could be at risk if I ignore it. Though it's inconvenient, I head to the service station to refill the air. I notice the difference every time: my car rides smoothly and drives better once the tires are properly inflated.

Life works similarly. The pressures we face may frustrate us, wear us down, or even shake our faith, but they are necessary. Pressure stretches us, strengthens us, and prepares us for God's greater glory. As Theodore Roosevelt once said, *"Nothing in the world worth having or doing comes easy."*

God knows just how much pressure we can handle. He knows when to release it, when to increase it, and how to use it for our good. Psalm 34:18, ESV assures us that "The Lord is near to the brokenhearted and saves the crushed in spirit." Even when life feels overwhelming, we are never left to endure it alone.

Jesus Himself experienced ultimate pressure when He bore the weight of our sins on Calvary. The crushing weight of the cross was more than any of us could endure, but He took it for us. Because of His sacrifice, we can find strength and peace in our own moments of pressure.

So, the next time the "pressure light" of life comes on, don't ignore it. Let it remind you that God is at work, using every ounce of pressure to draw you closer to Him and to shape you for His glory.

Prayer:

Lord, thank You for being present with me during the pressures of life. Help me not to resist or resent pressure, but to trust that You are using it to strengthen me. Remind me of Jesus' sacrifice when I feel overwhelmed and teach me to rely on Your sustaining grace.

Amen

Lessons of Faith and Grace

Reflecting Questions:

1. In what areas of your life do you currently feel the greatest "pressure," and how might God be using it to protect or prepare you?
2. How does remembering that Jesus endured the ultimate pressure at the cross give you hope when you feel weary or close to breaking?
3. Instead of viewing pressure only as frustration, what practices can help you see it as an opportunity to lean more fully on God's strength?

TRUST HIM WITH THE "SOCCER TURN"

My Bible reads: *"Trust in the Lord with all your heart, and do not lean on your own understanding. In all your ways acknowledge him, and he will make straight your paths."* - Proverbs 3:5–6, ESV

Reflection

While attending my daughter's soccer game, I noticed how often the crowd shouted, *"Turn it!"* In soccer, turning is a crucial skill, as it enables players to maneuver away from defenders and position themselves for a successful pass or goal.

As I reflected on the game, I realized how much the concept of turning applies to our walk with God. He is the ultimate playmaker, turning our situations around in ways we often don't expect. Sometimes, He turns us away from what looks promising, only to lead us toward something better. Sometimes His turn feels uncomfortable, but it is always purposeful.

The Bible is filled with examples of divine turns. The woman with the issue of blood experienced a complete turnaround the moment she touched the hem of Jesus' garment (Matthew 9:22). Peter, who once denied Christ, was later restored and entrusted with leading the church

(Luke 22:54–62). God specializes in turning brokenness into blessing.

But trusting the "turn" requires surrender. Trusting God doesn't mean He'll do things the way we want; it means being at peace with how He chooses to work. It means recognizing that His ways are higher than ours, and His wisdom surpasses our understanding.

Just as a soccer player must trust the coach's strategy and the timing of the turn, we must trust God's plan for our lives. There is freedom, peace, and victory when we release control and let Him direct our paths.

Prayer:

Lord, thank You for being the One who turns my situations around for good. Help me to trust You with every turn in life, even when I don't understand it. Teach me to rest in Your sovereignty, listen to Your Spirit, and rejoice in the victories You have planned for me.

Amen

Annette Richardson

Reflecting Questions:

1. In what areas of your life do you feel God is asking you to "turn" away from the defender (the distractions, doubts, or fears) and trust Him with the outcome?
2. How does Proverbs 3:5–6 challenge you to release your own understanding and lean fully into God's direction when His ways don't match your plans?
3. What step of obedience is God calling you to take right now that requires trusting His "pass" and His timing, even if you can't yet see the goal?

WHEN APPLES FALL

My Bible reads: *"You will recognize them by their fruits. Are grapes gathered from thornbushes, or figs from thistles?"* - Matthew 7:16, ESV

Reflection

We've all heard the saying, *"The apple doesn't fall far from the tree."* Parents are like apple trees, and their children are the fruit. Just as apples carry the qualities of the tree they grow from, children often carry the values, habits, and teachings of their parents.

Apples vary; some are sweet, some are tart, some are large, others are small. But every apple is identified by the tree that produced it. Likewise, Jesus tells us that people are known by their fruit (Matthew 7:16). A good tree produces good fruit, while a bad tree produces bad fruit. Parents influence their children, but children also reflect on the "tree" that raised them.

As I reflect on my own life, I am reminded of the lessons my mother instilled in me. The greatest of all was the importance of having a relationship with Jesus. She taught me that apart from Him, nothing is possible. John 15:5, ESV reminds us, "I am the vine; you are the branches. Whoever abides in me and I in him, he it is that bears much fruit, for apart from me you can do nothing."

Because my mother was rooted in Christ, her life produced good fruit. And because she taught me to stay connected to the Vine, I, too, bear fruit that reflects her faith and her God. Strength, grace, love, hope, generosity, these are the apples that fell from her tree. When our apples fall, may they be found close to the Vine, reflecting the life of Jesus Christ.

Prayer:

Lord, thank You for the people who planted seeds of faith in my life. Help me to stay connected to You, the true Vine, so that I may produce fruit that glorifies You. May my life yield good fruit that blesses others and points them to Christ.

Amen

Lessons of Faith and Grace

Reflecting Questions:

1. What kind of "fruit" are you producing in your life right now, and how does it reflect your connection to Jesus, the True Vine (John 15:5)?
2. Which values or lessons passed down to you, by parents, mentors, or spiritual guides, most shape the way you live today?
3. If someone were to "taste" the fruit of your life, what would they say it reveals about your faith and relationship with Christ?

FINDING STRENGTH IN CONNECTION

My Bible reads: "For if they fall, one will lift up his fellow. But woe to him who is alone when he falls and has not another to lift him up!" - Ecclesiastes 4:10, ESV

Reflection

Before every cross-country meet, my son has a ritual. He pressed his forehead against mine and looked directly into my eyes. In that moment, I know he is searching for me, for encouragement, for peace, and for the assurance that I am right there with him. That simple gesture speaks louder than words. It's a sacred pause where love, support, and trust are exchanged without saying a thing.

As I reflect on those moments, I am reminded of how our Heavenly Father longs for us to press close to Him before we face the "meets" of life. Just as my son draws strength from that connection, we are called to draw our strength from God. My Bible also reads, "Draw near to God, and He will draw near to you" (James 4:8, ESV). When life feels daunting, we don't have to face it alone. We can lean into Him, knowing His presence brings courage and calm.

In every race, whether we win or lose, the nearness of God gives us the confidence to endure. My Bible reads again, "but they who wait for the Lord shall renew their strength; they shall mount up with wings like eagles; they shall run and not be weary; they shall walk and not faint." (Isaiah 40:31, ESV). Just like my son seeks my steady gaze, we too must lift our eyes to the One who promises never to leave us or forsake us.

Before your next challenge, whether it's a meeting, a conversation, or a season of uncertainty, pause. Press your heart to His, seek His face, and receive the strength He so freely offers.

Prayer:

Lord, thank You for the precious reminders You give us through simple moments. Just as children look to parents to find comfort, strength, and reassurance, help me to press close to You each day. Teach me to draw near before every challenge, every "race," and every trial I face. Fill me with Your peace, strengthen my spirit, and steady my steps. May I always run with endurance, fixing my eyes on Jesus, the Author and Finisher of my faith. Thank You for being my constant source of encouragement and strength.

Amen

Annette Richardson

Reflecting Questions:

1. When was the last time you intentionally drew near to God before facing a challenge?
2. How do you usually prepare for life's "races?" With worry, or with prayer and trust?
3. How can you practice pausing and seeking God's presence before entering your daily responsibilities or trials?

Lessons of Faith and Grace

CHAPTER 3:
Strength and Grace in Trials

Life brings seasons of pressure, loss, and unanswered questions. Yet in the valley, God proves Himself faithful. In the following stories, you will learn what it means to endure hardship while holding fast to faith, hope, joy, and the grace of God. We are reminded that God never wastes our pain. He is the One who strengthens, refines, and transforms us through every trial.

FAITH THAT MOVES MOUNTAINS

My Bible reads: *"for we walk by faith, not by sight."*
- 2 Corinthians 5:7, ESV

Reflection

God will always do what He has promised to do in our lives. Our role is to have faith; not just ordinary faith, but audacious faith that believes He will exceed our expectations. When challenges arise, our first response should be faith, not fear. Faith pleases God and positions us to receive His best. James 1:3 tells us that trials come to test and perfect our faith. In those moments, we must hold on to the truth that God is omnipotent and faithful to His Word.

Faith also involves what we speak. Proverbs 18:21, ESV reminds us that "death and life are in the power of the tongue." Our words have creative power, they can build up or tear down. When we face obstacles, we must speak life, declare God's promises, and command the "mountains" to move.

My Bible reads in Mark 11:23, ESV, "Truly, I say to you, whoever says to this mountain, 'Be taken up and thrown into the sea,' and does not doubt in his heart, but believes that what he says will come to pass, it will be done for him." Faith is not passive, it acts, speaks, and expects.

Faith purifies our hearts, strengthens our minds, and removes the mountains of guilt, fear, and doubt that try to block us. No obstacle is too great for the God who lives within us.

Prayer:

Lord, strengthen my faith so that I respond with confidence instead of fear. Help me to speak life over every situation, to believe Your promises, and to trust You even when I cannot see the outcome. Teach me to live with audacious faith that moves mountains.

Amen

Lessons of Faith and Grace

Reflecting Questions:

1. What "mountains" (obstacles, challenges, or fears) are you currently facing, and how might God be calling you to approach them with faith instead of doubt?
2. How does remembering that God is both present *during the climb* and powerful enough to *move the mountain* encourage you to persevere?
3. In what ways can you practice speaking God's Word over the "mountains" in your life, trusting Him to bring a breakthrough in His time?

IT IS PART OF THE PROCESS

My Bible reads: *"But all things should be done decently and in order."* - 1 Corinthians 14:40, ESV

Reflection

In the final days of my mother's life, she would often ask me about the changes happening in her body. "Annette, why are my arms so small?" "Annette, why am I short of breath?" She knew she was dying, though those words are never easy to hear. Together, we decided to reframe it with a phrase: *"It's part of the process."*

Life is full of processes. Some are joyful–like raising children, learning new skills, or baking a cake. Others are painful, like loss, grief, or transition. But whether pleasant or painful, every process has a purpose.

David knew this well. In the Psalms, he wrestled with grief, fear, anger, and betrayal. Yet in the process of those emotions, David leaned into God–his source of strength. He didn't skip steps or pretend away the pain. He let the process shape him, drawing him closer to the Lord.

So often, we want to rush through seasons that hurt or skip steps that feel uncomfortable. But God's process is intentional. Every season (even the ones we wish we could bypass) is designed to grow our faith, character, wisdom, strength, and endurance.

For my mom, her process led her home to Jesus. For us still here, our processes can lead us into deeper communion with Him if we will trust His hand. When we choose to surrender instead of resist, we discover that His strength is enough to carry us through.

Prayer:

Lord, thank You for being with me in every process of life. Help me to trust You when the steps feel hard or confusing. Give me patience not to rush ahead and faith to believe that You are working all things for my good. Teach me to embrace the process and grow closer to You through it.

Amen

Reflecting Questions:

1. When you think about the "processes" in your own life, whether growth, loss, or change, what steps has God used to shape your faith and character?
2. Which part of your current process are you most tempted to resist or rush, and how might trusting God's timing bring you peace?
3. Looking back, how have past processes (even painful ones) revealed lessons, strength, or blessings that you could not see in the moment?

BREAKING AND BECOMING

My Bible reads: *"And we know that for those who love God all things work together for good, for those who are called according to his purpose."*
- Romans 8:28, ESV

Reflection

2018 was one of the most difficult years of my life. Within the same season, I experienced the transition of my mother to her Heavenly home and the ending of my marriage. Both events left me feeling shattered and uncertain about what life would look like moving forward. There were days when getting out of bed required more strength than I thought I had. Grief and heartbreak visited me daily, and I often felt like I was walking through a fog that refused to lift. But even in the midst of my pain, I could feel God's hand holding me together when everything else seemed to fall apart.

My Bible reads, "The Lord is near to the brokenhearted and saves the crushed in spirit." (Psalm 34:18, ESV). I clung to this verse as a lifeline. I began to understand that seasons of breaking are often God's way of preparing us for becoming. While I lost two of the most significant relationships in my life that year, I found a deeper, more intimate relationship with my Heavenly Father. In the quiet moments of loneliness, He spoke peace to my heart. When tears flowed without warning, He whispered promises of restoration and purpose.

God never wastes our pain. What felt like the end of my story was actually the beginning of a new chapter–one filled with growth, self-discovery, and an unwavering faith that could only be forged in the fire of adversity. I am a witness that even when everything familiar is stripped away, God remains constant, faithful, and kind.

When I reflect on 2018, I no longer see it as the year I lost everything. I see it as the year I found God in a way I never had before. It was the year I learned that He truly gives beauty for ashes and joy for mourning.

Prayer:

Lord, thank You for being my strength in seasons of loss and my anchor in the storm. When life breaks my heart, remind me that You are the potter, and I am the clay; even my broken pieces are safe in Your hands. Help me to trust Your process when I cannot see the outcome, and to find peace in knowing that You are always working for my good. Restore my joy, renew my hope, and help me to see that through every ending, You are creating something new.

Amen

Reflecting Questions:

1. What season (or event) in your life felt like everything was falling apart, and how did you experience God's presence in the middle of it?
2. How can you begin to view your times of loss or heartache as opportunities for spiritual growth rather than defeat?
3. Romans 8:28 reminds us that God works all things for our good. What "good" has come from a painful season in your life that you didn't see at the time?

IT'S THE PIERCING FOR ME

My Bible reads: *"But one of the soldiers pierced his side with a spear, and at once there came out blood and water."* - John 19:34, ESV

Reflection

In March 2020, I decided to get my nose pierced. I did my research, found a hygienic business, and walked in nervous but determined. The young lady who helped me was kind and reassuring–she said, "You'll be *fine*." A moment later, I heard a loud click, felt a sharp pain, and tears and blood flowed down my nose. My daughter recorded the whole process, laughing and asking if I was okay. For the record, I would never do it again!

That piercing, though temporary and cosmetic, reminds me of a much greater piercing–the one Jesus endured for us. During the Easter season, it's easy to get caught up in bunnies, egg hunts, and dinners, but we must not forget the piercing that changed eternity.

When the soldier pierced Jesus' side, both blood and water flowed out. The blood dealt with our sins, washing us clean and reconciling us to God. The water signified life–life imparted into us through His sacrifice. Because of His piercing, we are forgiven, redeemed, and free.

It's the piercing for me: the one that brought salvation, healing, and eternal hope. Let us not allow the world's distractions to overshadow the power of the cross.

Prayer:

Lord, thank You for the sacrifice of Jesus, who endured the piercing for me. Thank You for the blood that cleanses my sins and the living water that gives me new life. Help me to focus on Your redemptive power this resurrection season and always walk in gratitude for the cross.

Amen

Reflecting Questions:

1. When you think about the physical pain of a piercing compared to the suffering of Christ, how does it deepen your gratitude for the sacrifice He made for you?
2. Jesus' side was pierced, and both blood and water flowed out (John 19:34). What does the significance of the blood (forgiveness of sins) and the water (new life) mean to you personally?
3. In what ways can you keep your focus on the cross during Easter or any season so that Christ's sacrifice remains the center of your worship rather than worldly distractions?

THE GIFT OF LAUGHTER: GOD'S MEDICINE FOR THE SOUL

My Bible reads: *"A joyful heart is good medicine, but a crushed spirit dries up the bones."*
- Proverbs 17:22, ESV

Reflection

In November 2014, my mom called a family meeting with my sisters and me. She shared the news that she had found a lump in her breast. At first, you might think we would cry, but instead, we laughed. I am not sure why we laughed and though it may have seemed strange, I believe that laughter was God's way of strengthening us in that moment.

Throughout her illness, laughter became a vital part of our journey. We told stories, teased each other, and found joy in the small things. Humor became medicine for our souls. My Bible reads in Job 8:21 that God will fill your mouth with laughter and your lips with shouts of joy. I believe He did exactly that for us.

Laughter doesn't erase pain, but it lightens the load. It reminds us not to take life so seriously that we forget the joy God offers us, even in trials. Robert Frost once said, *"If we could not laugh, we would go insane."* For my family, laughter was a lifeline, a way to cope, and a way to hold onto joy even as we faced loss.

So, I encourage you, laugh often. Laugh when life feels heavy. Laugh when it feels like you are drowning. Laughter won't solve your problems, but it will strengthen your spirit and help you keep going.

Prayer:

Lord, thank You for the gift of laughter. Thank You for the way it strengthens, heals, and reminds us of Your joy. Help me to find moments of laughter even in difficult seasons, and let my joy be a testimony of Your goodness.

Amen

Reflecting Questions:

1. When has God used laughter in your life to bring strength, healing, or relief during a difficult season?
2. Proverbs 17:22, ESV says, "A joyful heart is good medicine." How can you intentionally cultivate joy and humor in your daily walk with God, even when life feels heavy?
3. Laughter helped me and my family endure my mother's illness. Who in your life might need the gift of laughter from you today, and how could you share it with them?

FINDING SHALOM

My Bible reads: *"Peace I leave with you; my peace I give to you. Not as the world gives do I give to you. Let not your hearts be troubled, neither let them be afraid."* - John 14:27, ESV

Reflection

The Hebrew word *shalom* means peace, but it is so much more than the absence of conflict. Shalom speaks of wholeness, completeness, and well-being. When peace reigns in our hearts, we can stand bold and steadfast even in the face of adversity.

Peace is not circumstantial; it is divine. It doesn't come from perfect conditions or smooth paths but from knowing Jesus, the Prince of Peace. Isaiah 9:6 reminds us that His reign of peace is supreme and enduring. Jesus Himself said, "I have said these things to you, that in me you may have peace. In the world you will have tribulation. But take heart; I have overcome the world." (John 16:33, ESV). His peace is durable, not fleeting.

When our thoughts race and our anxieties rise, God invites us to cast our cares on Him (1 Peter 5:7). By surrendering our worries, we make room for His shalom to rule in our minds, hearts, and souls. This peace doesn't deny our struggles; it steadies us in them.

Shalom is both a gift and a responsibility. It is something we receive from God and something we nurture by living true to Him and to ourselves. In Christ, peace is not just something we hope to find in eternity; it is a reality we can experience now.

Prayer:

Lord, thank You for being my Prince of Peace. Teach me to trust You with every worry and to rest in the shalom You offer. Fill my heart with Your perfect peace so that I may live boldly and steadfastly in every season of life.

Amen

Reflecting Questions:

1. Jesus said, "Peace I leave with you; my peace I give to you" (John 14:27, ESV). How does this promise of durable, God-given peace change the way you face fear, uncertainty, or difficult circumstances?
2. What tends to steal your peace most often, fear, busyness, conflict, or worry? How can you invite God's perfect Shalom into those areas of your life?
3. Isaiah 9:6 reminds us that Christ is the Prince of Peace. What practical steps can you take each day to stay rooted in Him, rather than depending on external conditions for your peace?

THE MISSING

My Bible reads: *"The Lord is not slow to fulfill his promise as some count slowness, but is patient toward you, not wishing that any should perish, but that all should reach repentance."* - 2 Peter 3:9, ESV

Reflection

According to NAMUS, about 60,000 people go missing in the United States each year, and over 4,000 unidentified bodies are recovered. Tragically, my father is one of those missing. On December 12, 2012, he disappeared.

For nearly seven years, my sisters and I searched for answers. The pain of not knowing has been an indescribable torment, a nightmare without closure. I still glance at my phone sometimes, hoping it will ring and I'll hear his voice on the other end. My father was strong, loving, and a man who shaped my heart for reading, writing, and compassion. His absence has left a permanent ache.

My longing for my earthly father reminds me of the heart of our Heavenly Father. He, too, is burdened for those who are lost. Every soul matters to Him. Every wandering child is missed. Just as my family has searched for my dad, God seeks after His children. He is not willing that any should perish, but longs for all to come home to Him.

Most people won't care about how much we know about God until they know how much we care. Our compassion for the "missing" (those far from God) is how He reaches *them* through *us*. We are called to pray, to share, and to love the lost into the arms of Jesus.

Prayer:

Lord, thank You for being a Father who searches for the missing and longs for the lost to return home. Teach me to carry Your burden for those who don't yet know You. Fill me with compassion, courage, and love so that I may reflect Your heart to others. And thank You for holding me close even in the ache of my own missing.

Amen

Reflecting Questions:

1. How has experiencing (or imagining) the pain of a missing loved one given you greater compassion for God's heart toward those who are spiritually lost?
2. 2 Peter 3:9 reminds us that God is "not willing that any should perish." How does this verse challenge you to pray for, serve, or reach out to those who don't yet know Him?
3. What practical steps can you take to grow in sensitivity toward "the missing" around you, those who may be overlooked, forgotten, or far from God?

CHAPTER 4:
Faithful Stewardship

God has entrusted each of us with gifts, relationships, and responsibilities that require care, discipline, and gratitude. Stewardship is not limited to finances or ministry; it encompasses the way we care for every aspect of our lives. In the following stories, we are reminded that our health, our children, and our everyday choices are sacred opportunities to honor God. Stewardship is worship in action. These stories inspire us to see self-care not as selfishness but as obedience, parenting not as control but as partnership with God, and wellness not as vanity but as reverence. True stewardship flows from gratitude and leads to grace.

TEMPLE MAINTENANCE

My Bible reads: *"Or do you not know that your body is a temple of the Holy Spirit within you, whom you have from God? You are not your own, for you were bought with a price. So glorify God in your body."*
- 1 Corinthians 6:19-20, ESV

Reflection

In recent years, I was told that I was pre-diabetic. I also noticed the number on the scale slowly creeping upward. As a nurse, I understood the medical implications of neglecting my health, yet I found myself in a cycle of fatigue, unhealthy eating, and stress. Somewhere between taking care of family and others, I had stopped taking care of myself.

It's interesting how often those of us who serve other medical professionals, caregivers, and even church folks neglect the very vessel God gave us to carry out His work. We pray for healing and strength, yet ignore the wisdom and discipline that God has already given us to maintain our health.

We cannot be so spiritual that we neglect the physical. God expects us to care for the body He designed through rest, nourishment, movement, and balance. Just as we make time for prayer and devotion, we must also make time to walk, drink water, and eat foods that sustain life. Stewardship is not just about money or ministry; it's about managing every gift God has given us, including our health.

The truth is, our spiritual calling can only thrive when our physical health supports it. When we are unwell, our energy, focus, and endurance for God's work are compromised. My Bible reads that prosperity in health is part of God's desire for His children. It is not about vanity, but vitality, the strength to do what He has called us to do.

I am learning that honoring God with my body is not about perfection but progression. It's about saying "yes" to small, consistent changes, taking the stairs, and setting boundaries for rest. When we treat our bodies as holy vessels, we give God glory not only in our worship but also in our wellness.

Prayer:

Lord, thank You for the gift of my body and the life You breathe into me each day. Forgive me for the times I have neglected the care of this temple You entrusted to me. Help me to make wise choices, to move my body with joy, and to nourish it with gratitude. Teach me balance, discipline, and self-control so that I can serve

You with strength and energy. Let my wellness be a reflection of Your grace at work in me.

Amen

Reflecting Questions:

1. In what ways have you neglected caring for the body God has entrusted to you, and what small changes can you begin making today to restore balance and health?
2. How does viewing your body as a *temple of the Holy Spirit* change your motivation toward eating, exercise, and rest?
3. How can you encourage others, especially those in caregiving or ministry roles, to honor God through better self-care and stewardship of their health?

PARENTING THROUGH THE SEASONS

My Bible reads: *"All your children shall be taught by the Lord, and great shall be the peace of your children."* - Isaiah 54:13, ESV

Reflection

Parenting is one of the most humbling and holy assignments God has ever entrusted to me. From the moment I held my children in my arms, I realized that my life would never be the same. I was responsible for nurturing, protecting, and guiding another soul, a task both beautiful and terrifying. What I did not realize then was that parenting, much like life, comes in seasons.

There was the baby season, filled with sleepless nights and tender cuddles. The elementary years brought scraped knees, homework, and endless questions. The teenage years tested my patience and deepened my prayer life. Now, as my children transition into adulthood, I've learned that parenting never truly ends; it simply changes form. I am still their mother, but my role has shifted from hands-on guidance to heartfelt intercession.

My Bible reads, "Train up a child in the way he should go; even when he is old he will not depart from it."

(Proverbs 22:6, ESV). This verse reminds me that while I cannot walk every road for them, I can plant seeds that will lead them back to the path of righteousness when life tries to pull them away. Parenting is not about perfection; it is about persistence, showing up in prayer, love, and faith, even when you do not see immediate results.

Every stage of parenting requires surrender. When they were small, I had to surrender my time. When they were teenagers, I had to surrender my control. Now that they are adults, I surrender my expectations and trust that God's hand will guide them just as He has guided me. What peace it brings to know that God Himself is teaching them lessons I never could.

Parenting through the seasons has taught me that God is not only working within my children, but He is also working within me. Through every prayer, tear, proud moment, and hard goodbye, He is shaping me into the parent He designed me to be.

Prayer:

Lord, thank You for the gift of my children and for the privilege of walking beside them through every stage of life. Help me to release control and trust You with their hearts, their choices, and their futures. Give me wisdom to guide them, patience to love them, and faith to surrender them into Your hands. Remind me that

You love them even more than I do, and that You are writing a beautiful story through their lives.

Amen

Annette Richardson

Reflecting Questions:

1. How has your role as a parent changed through the different seasons of your children's lives, and what has each stage taught you about God's character?
2. In what ways can you surrender control and trust God more fully with your children's growth, choices, and future?
3. What can you do today to express love and encouragement to your children, no matter their age or stage in life? How can you intentionally plant seeds of faith in your children's lives through prayer, words, and action, that will continue to bear fruit long after they are grown?

SEEDS OF ACCESS

My Bible reads: *"Children, obey your parents in the Lord, for this is right. "Honor your father and mother" (this is the first commandment with a promise), "that it may go well with you and that you may live long in the land."* - Ephesians 6:1–3, ESV

Reflections

I often think about how my mother and father influenced the person I am today. Their lessons, prayers, and sacrifices continue to shape my life, even long after their voices have quieted. Honoring my parents has not always been easy, especially when life presented challenges or differences of opinion, but over time, I've learned that honoring them is not just about obedience; it's about access. Honoring our parents opens doors that disobedience and dishonor will close.

My Bible reads, "Honor your father and your mother, that your days may be long upon the land which the Lord your God is giving you." (Exodus 20:12). This commandment is not a suggestion; it is a principle. God designed honor as a seed, a spiritual law that yields divine access to blessings, favor, and longevity. When we show respect, gratitude, and love toward our parents, we are sowing into the soil of God's promises.

Sometimes, we think honoring our parents means agreeing with everything they say or do, but true honor transcends perfection. It is about recognizing their role in God's plan for our lives. Even if our parents made mistakes and most have, God can still use our honor toward them as a pathway for healing, reconciliation, and blessing.

When I look back over my life, I can see that many of my open doors were tied to the seeds of honor I planted early on through service, forgiveness, and respect. Even small acts of kindness toward my parents bore fruit later in ways I never expected. Honor has a voice that reaches Heaven. It speaks when we pray, when we give, and even when we forgive.

Honoring our parents is not only about them, but also about positioning ourselves to receive what God desires to release into our lives. Honor is a key that unlocks favor. It is a seed that gives access to divine inheritance. When we sow it, we tap into the generational blessings that God designed to flow through families.

Prayer:

Lord, thank You for the parents You chose for me. Help me to honor them in both word and deed, even when it's difficult. Teach me to see them as You see them as vessels through whom You brought life and purpose into the world. Let my acts of honor become seeds that open doors of favor, peace, and restoration. Heal any brokenness in my heart and give me a spirit of gratitude for the gift of family. May my life reflect the legacy of honor that brings You glory.

Amen

Reflecting Questions:

1. What specific ways can you honor your parents, whether through words, actions, or prayer, regardless of your current relationship with them?
2. How does understanding honor as a "seed of access" change the way you view the blessings and opportunities in your own life?
3. How can you model the principle of honor for the next generation so that your children or those you influence learn to value it as well?

Lessons of Faith and Grace

CHAPTER 5:
Celebrating God's Goodness

Our God is worthy of celebration!
He is generous with blessings, faithful to His promises, and ever-present in our lives.
In the following stories, cultivating gratitude, joy, and worship are illuminated.
These stories call us to celebrate God's goodness, with our words, our actions, and even our claps of praise. May you rejoice in and reflect on the faithfulness of a good and gracious God.

LOVE "AGAPE" STYLE

My Bible reads: *"so that Christ may dwell in your hearts through faith—that you, being rooted and grounded in love, may have strength to comprehend with all the saints what is the breadth and length and height and depth, and to know the love of Christ that surpasses knowledge, that you may be filled with all the fullness of God."* - Ephesians 3:17–19, ESV

Reflection

We all have a style, whether it's in the food we enjoy, the clothes we wear, or the way we do our hair. But beyond every fashion or trend, there's one style that surpasses them all: *agape-style love.*

Agape love is God's love. It's pure, selfless, and unconditional, the highest form of love. It's mentioned more than 100 times in the New Testament, showing its importance in the Christian life. Agape love is what we must extend not only to friends and family, but even to our enemies.

So, how do we love "Agape" style?

1. **Sacrifice** - Giving without expecting anything in return. The greatest example is God giving His only Son to die for our sins. Ask yourself: *What have I sacrificed for someone lately?*

2. **Showcase** - Demonstrating agape love in everyday moments. Learn to forgive quickly, wait patiently, choose kindness, and refrain from gossip. Even in inconveniences like long lines or delays, God gives us opportunities to showcase His love.
3. **Service** - Love is expressed through serving others. Jesus humbled Himself, washed His disciples' feet, and modeled true servanthood. Serving is not about being seen but about reflecting the heart of Christ.

Without love, our deeds lose their meaning. As C.S. Lewis said, *"Though our feelings come and go, God's love does not."* Agape love is powerful, restorative, healing, forgiving, and eternal.

Prayer:

Lord, thank You for loving me with an everlasting, unconditional love. Teach me to love like You with sacrifice, kindness, patience, and a servant's heart. Help me to showcase Your agape love in my words and actions, so that others may see Christ in me.

Amen

Reflecting Questions:

1. Where in your life can you begin to show agape love (sacrificial, unconditional) and selfless love even when it costs you something or when nothing is given in return?
2. How can you showcase agape love in everyday situations, like waiting patiently, forgiving quickly, or choosing not to gossip?
3. What does serving others with a heart like Jesus look like in your current season of life, and how might God be calling you to step into that kind of service?

THE CLIMB AND THE PROMISES

My Bible reads: *"And Jesus answered them, "Truly, I say to you, if you have faith and do not doubt, you will not only do what has been done to the fig tree, but even if you say to this mountain, 'Be taken up and thrown into the sea,' it will happen."*
- Matthew 21:21, ESV

Reflection

One of my favorite songs is *"Made a Way"* by Travis Greene. The lyrics remind me that God is a mountain mover:

"You move mountains.
You cause walls to fall,
With Your power;
Perform miracles.
There is nothing impossible.
And we're standing here,
Only because You made a way."

This song makes my heart smile because I can testify, God has moved mountains in my life.

Mountains represent obstacles, difficulties, and perplexities in my life. Whether it's illness, financial struggles, family challenges, or societal pressures, we all face mountains. But the joy of mountain climbing is this: we are never climbing alone. God promises to be with us, to strengthen us, and to reward those who seek Him in faith. Hebrews 11:6 reminds us that without faith, it is impossible to please God, and with faith, nothing is impossible.

Sometimes we miss seeing mountains move because we do not ask, or we do not truly believe. But when we approach God in faith, trusting His Word, He is faithful to respond. He can perform miracles and make a way when there seems to be no way.

I encourage you today to identify your mountains. Name them in prayer, place them before God, and believe that He can move them. There is nothing too big, too heavy, or too impossible for Him.

Prayer:

Lord, thank You for being the mountain mover in my life. Help me to face every obstacle with faith instead of fear. Teach me to trust Your power, believe Your Word, and stand firm knowing that nothing is impossible for You.

Amen

Reflecting Questions:

1. What "mountains" in your life feel immovable right now, and how can you bring them before God with faith that He is able to move them?
2. How does the promise in Hebrews 11:6, that God rewards those who diligently seek Him, encourage you to keep climbing even when the path feels steep?
3. When you look back on past "mountains" that God has helped you overcome, how does that history of His faithfulness strengthen your trust for today's challenges?

THE GOLF CLAP

My Bible reads: *"Clap your hands, all peoples! Shout to God with loud songs of joy!"* - Psalm 47:1, ESV

Reflection

When my daughter began playing on her high school golf team, I quickly learned the importance of golf etiquette. Spectators must stay still and quiet as players prepare their shots. To avoid distraction, applause is kept light, the famous "golf clap." It's subtle but meaningful, a way to celebrate without disrupting.

As I think about the golf clap, I'm reminded of the value of celebrating others. Whether it's a quiet gesture or a loud cheer, celebration matters. It uplifts, affirms, and acknowledges the victories of those around us.

More importantly, we are called to celebrate the victories of Jesus. Psalm 47:1 invites us to clap our hands and shout to God with triumph. Celebration is not only for sporting events; it is our worship response to a Savior who has redeemed us, protected us, and sustained us.

Even creation celebrates. Psalm 98:8, ESV says, "Let the rivers clap their hands; let the hills sing for joy together." If rivers and mountains, silent, immovable forces of nature, can exalt the Lord, how much more should we?

Celebration is in our spiritual DNA. Whether through clapping, dancing, lifting hands, or offering praise, we are created to celebrate the beauty and grandeur of God. And as we celebrate Him, we should also celebrate the people He places in our lives, honoring their victories, both great and small.

Prayer:

Lord, thank You for giving me reasons to celebrate daily. Teach me to clap, shout, sing, and rejoice in Your goodness. Help me to celebrate not only Your victories in my life but also the victories in the lives of others. May my heart be full of gratitude and my life full of praise.

Amen

Lessons of Faith and Grace

Reflecting Questions:

1. In your own life, how do you celebrate the victories of others; with a quiet "golf clap" or with a louder cheer? How might God be inviting you to be more intentional in affirming others?
2. Psalm 47:1, ESV reminds us to "clap your hands, all you people; shout to God with the voice of triumph." What does it look like for you personally to celebrate God's goodness with joy and freedom?
3. Just as rivers and hills "clap their hands" in praise (Psalm 98:8), what everyday parts of creation remind you to stop and give thanks to God?

OPEN HANDS, GOD'S PLANS

My Bible reads: *"For my thoughts are not your thoughts, neither are your ways my ways, declares the Lord. For as the heavens are higher than the earth, so are my ways higher than your ways and my thoughts than your thoughts."*
- Isaiah 55:8–9, ESV

Reflection

I recently spent a Sunday evening on the farm with my dear friend Rebecca, a woman I've been blessed to know for over ten years. Rebecca is kind, patient, poised, and honest, a straight shooter who has supported me through many seasons of life. Time on the farm is never wasted. Whether it's fresh eggs, vegetables, or her treasured words of wisdom, I always leave carrying something valuable.

During our time together, we laughed, shared stories, and even watched my daughter and son practice hitting golf balls. Later, as we sat in Rebecca's kitchen, she began talking about God's plans for our lives. She showed me her closed fist and said, "Do not fold your hands like this, because God has a plan." Then she opened her hand and said, "Hold your hand open, because when you hold too tightly, things, your plans, will not slip through your fingers."

Her point was simple but powerful: we need to release our grip on our own plans and let God be God in our lives. No matter how carefully we plan, His ways always rise above ours. Trusting God requires open hands and a surrendered heart. When we cling too tightly to our own agenda, we risk missing the greater plan He has prepared for us.

Prayer:

Lord, thank You that Your plans are higher and better than mine. Help me to open my hands, release control, and trust You with every detail of my life. Teach me to walk in faith, knowing that Your way is always best.

Amen

Reflecting Questions:

1. Isaiah 55:8–9 reminds us that God's thoughts and ways are higher than ours. In what areas of your life do you find it hardest to release your own plans and trust Him?
2. Rebecca's wisdom about holding your hands open was a picture of surrender. What might you be holding onto too tightly right now, and how can you practice opening your hands before God?
3. Looking back over your life, when has God's plan turned out better than your own, even if it didn't make sense in the moment? How does that history help you trust Him now?

I AM PROUD OF YOU

My Bible reads: *"Gracious words are like a honeycomb, sweetness to the soul and health to the body."* - Proverbs 16:24, ESV

Reflection

In May of 2017, I walked across the stage to receive my master's degree in nursing. It was a day of accomplishment, sacrifice, and gratitude. My mother had planned to attend the ceremony, but she was hospitalized at the time.

The day before graduation, I visited her in her hospital room. As I was leaving, she called out, "Annette." I turned back, and she softly said, "I am proud of you." Those five words brought me to tears. She had told me before, but on that day, they carried a weight that I will treasure forever.

Words are powerful. They can build up or tear down, heal or wound. Proverbs 15:23, ESV reminds us, "To make an apt answer is a joy to a man, and a word in season, how good it is!" Kind words, spoken in the right season, can change someone's day or even their life.

My mother's words affirmed my hard work, sacrifice, and dedication. More than that, they reminded me of the importance of speaking life over others. As followers of Christ, we are called to use our words wisely, to encourage, uplift, and bless.

Every day presents opportunities to say something kind, uplifting, or affirming to the people around us. May we never withhold the power of encouragement, because someone may be waiting for those very words to keep pressing on.

Prayer:

Lord, thank You for the gift of words and the power they hold. Teach me to speak life into others, to encourage them, and to reflect Your love through kindness. Help me to never miss the chance to say the right word at the right time.

Amen

Lessons of Faith and Grace

Reflecting Questions:

1. Proverbs 16:24 says, "Gracious words are like a honeycomb, sweetness to the soul and health to the body." What words of encouragement or affirmation have most deeply impacted your life, and why?
2. How can you use your words this week to build someone up, especially someone who may feel unseen, unappreciated, or discouraged?
3. If you imagine God speaking over you, *"I am proud of you,"* how does that change the way you see yourself and live out your calling in Christ?

Author's Message

Looking back over the pages of this book, there is a common thread woven through every story: God's faithfulness. Whether in moments of joy or in seasons of grief, His hand has been present. His Word has been my anchor. His Spirit has been my comfort.

Through life's lessons, whether they came through my mother's wisdom, my children's experiences, or my own seasons of struggle, I have learned that God is nearby. He is the God of promises, the God of peace, the God of grace, and the God who turns sorrow into joy.

Every story told here points back to Him. Each reflection is not about me, but about the One who sustains me. Just as He has walked with me, I know He will walk with you. My prayer is that as you read, you were reminded that you are not alone. You are loved with an everlasting love. You are seen, heard, and cherished by your Heavenly Father.

Life is not without its valleys. We will experience loss, pain, and unanswered questions. Yet, amid it all, we can hold fast to the truth that God is faithful. His Word is trustworthy. His promises never fail. His love never ends.

So, take heart. Laugh when you can. Forgive freely. Love deeply. Live well. And above all, keep your eyes fixed on Jesus, the author and finisher of your faith.

www.ingramcontent.com/pod-product-compliance
Lightning Source LLC
Chambersburg PA
CBHW050247010526
44107CB00003B/212

9781970179187